Rob and Socks

by Kristin Cashore
illustrated by Bob Masheris

PEARSON

Scott
Foresman

Editorial Offices: Glenview, Illinois • Parsippany, New Jersey • New York, New York
Sales Offices: Needham, Massachusetts • Duluth, Georgia • Glenview, Illinois
Coppell, Texas • Ontario, California • Mesa, Arizona

Rob and Socks help Mom.

Rob and Socks help Mom with the hogs.

Socks was in the mud.

Rob and Socks use rocks to fix the wall.

Rob and Socks get to go to town.

Farm Dogs

Farm dogs do not have much time to play in the mud! Farm dogs have many jobs. They help the farmer herd the animals. They keep the animals safe from wolves and foxes. They stop animals from eating the crops. Farm dogs are hard workers!